D1117560

PRO WRESTLING'S GREATEST

SECRETS EXPOSED

BY MATT SCHEFF

SportsZone

An Imprint of Abdo Publishing
abdopublishing.com

abdopublishing.com

Published by Abdo Publishing, a division of ABDO, PO Box 398166, Minneapolis, Minnesota 55439. Copyright © 2017 by Abdo Consulting Group, Inc. International copyrights reserved in all countries. No part of this book may be reproduced in any form without written permission from the publisher. SportsZone™ is a trademark and logo of Abdo Publishing.

Printed in the United States of America, North Mankato, Minnesota
102016
012017

THIS BOOK CONTAINS
RECYCLED MATERIALS

Cover Photo: Paul Abell/WWE/AP Images
Interior Photos: Paul Abell/WWE/AP Images, 1; Max Blain/Shutterstock Images, 4-5; Alexandre Pona/Cityfiles/Icon Sportswire, 6-7; Tom "Mo" Moschella/Icon Sportswire, 8; Xinhua/Imago/Icon Sportswire, 9; Nhat V. Meyer/ZumaPress/Icon Sportswire, 10; Brandon Wade/WWE/AP Images, 11; Matt Roberts/ZumaPress/Icon Sportswire, 12-13; Michael Lipchitz/AP Images, 14; Ciao Hollywood/Splash Images/Newscom, 15; Chris Carlson/AP Images, 16-17; Mitrofanov Alexander/Shutterstock Images, 18-19; Erik S. Lesser/AP Images, 20; Tina Fineberg/AP Images, 21; Rick Mackler/ZumaPress/Newscom, 22-23; Gail Burton/AP Images, 24-25; Don Feria/WWE/AP Images, 26; John Palmer/MediaPunch/IPX/AP Images, 27; Marc Serota/AP Images, 28; Rick Scuteri/AP Images, 29

Editor: Patrick Donnelly
Series Designer: Laura Polzin

Publisher's Cataloging-in-Publication Data
Names: Scheff, Matt, author.
Title: Pro wrestling's greatest secrets exposed / by Matt Scheff.
Description: Minneapolis, MN : Abdo Publishing, 2017. | Series: Pro wrestling's greatest | Includes bibliographical references and index.
Identifiers: LCCN 2016945610 | ISBN 9781680784985 (lib. bdg.) | ISBN 9781680798265 (ebook)
Subjects: LCSH: Wrestling--Juvenile literature.
Classification: DDC 796.812--dc23
LC record available at http://lccn.loc.gov/2016945610

TABLE OF CONTENTS

INTRODUCTION: SHOWTIME!

The lights go down. The music blares. Cameras flash as the wrestlers make their way to the ring. The fans go wild. They know that they're about to see a great show. But what they don't see is all of the work that has gone into making this spectacle.

Wrestlers play to the fans at
the start of a match.

Fans mob Jeff Hardy at a match in Lisbon, Portugal.

A big-time pro wrestling show takes hundreds of people and countless hours to produce. Fans know about the long-running story lines and the wrestlers' personalities. But there's a lot going on that they never see, from the wrestlers' preparation to the behind-the-scenes work needed to pull it all off. Read on to learn more about pro wrestling's greatest secrets.

TEN

UNDERNEATH THE MAT

The mat is at the center of every match. But fans rarely pay much attention to it. Every mat is carefully built with safety in mind. It starts with a set of springs and steel beams. A stage of wooden planks lies on top of the springs. Soft foam goes over the wood. Finally, canvas is stretched over the foam. That's the top surface. The finished mat is firm, but cushioned.

Turnbuckles connect the ropes in each corner of the ring.

THE ROPES

A set of three ropes surrounds the ring. These ropes are flexible and springy. They are connected at each corner by turnbuckles. Wrestlers often climb these turnbuckles to launch high-flying moves at their opponents.

The ropes and mat are important parts of the wrestling ring.

Wrestling fans make plenty of noise, but sometimes they get help from sound systems.

NINE

CROWD NOISE

A wrestling arena is a noisy place. The crowd cheers and jeers the wrestlers in the ring. But did you know that not all of that sound comes from fans? Wrestling promoters often play extra sound over huge speakers. This "piped in" crowd noise helps to increase the level of excitement for the fans and wrestlers alike.

Massive sound systems help raise the noise level at arena shows.

EIGHT

WHAT'S IN A BELT?

Wrestling belts look like they're worth a million bucks. But in truth, they're much cheaper. Early belts were made from cardboard and tin. Today, belts are a little more solid. They're built out of leather and metal plates. The plates are often covered with a thin layer of gold to give them their shine. Simple belts can start at $1,000.

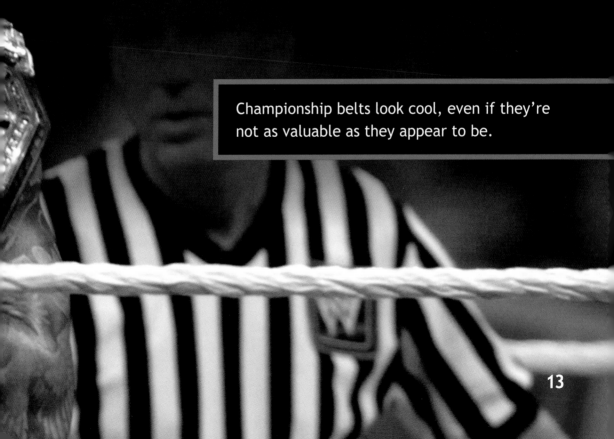

Championship belts look cool, even if they're not as valuable as they appear to be.

SEVEN

MULTISPORT STARS

Many wrestlers are world-class athletes. Some got their start in amateur wrestling. Kurt Angle won a gold medal in freestyle wrestling at the 1996 Olympics in Atlanta, Georgia. The Rock played football at the University of Miami. Meanwhile, Bill Goldberg spent time with the NFL's Atlanta Falcons. Randy Savage played minor league baseball. Many modern wrestlers have found success in mixed martial arts (MMA). Brock Lesnar won the Ultimate Fighting Championship (UFC) World Heavyweight championship in 2008.

Kurt Angle celebrates after winning the gold medal in the 100 kg (220 pound) weight class at the 1996 Olympics in Atlanta.

Dwayne "The Rock" Johnson has been a football player and an actor.

SIX

KAYFABE

Pro wrestlers often take on wild personalities. They know that fans love heroic babyfaces and terrible heels. Wrestlers use the term "kayfabe" to describe their characters' antics. Kayfabe is all about putting on an exciting show. An example is the relationship between wrestling legends Kane and The Undertaker. They play the roles of brothers. But they aren't actually brothers in real life. It was kayfabe to make an interesting story line.

Wrestlers such as Hulk Hogan create characters whose wild antics entertain their fans.

FIVE

HOUSE SHOWS

Many fans see pro wrestling TV shows and specials. But they might not realize that wrestlers do a lot of wrestling that most fans never see. House shows are traveling promotions. Wrestlers travel all around, putting on matches that never go on TV. The action in the ring is often great. But organizers are careful that nothing too important happens in house shows. Belts don't change hands. Rivalries don't begin or end. That's all saved for the on-screen action.

Many pro wrestling matches aren't made for TV audiences.

FOUR

THE WCW CHALLENGE

World Wrestling Entertainment (WWE) is king in modern pro wrestling. But that wasn't always the case. Starting in 1995, World Championship Wrestling (WCW) challenged WWE as the top promotion. WWE and WCW faced off in an epic battle called the Monday Night Wars. Both promotions aired their biggest shows on Monday night in a ratings war. For a time, it appeared that WCW would be the fans' choice. But WWE was the ultimate victor.

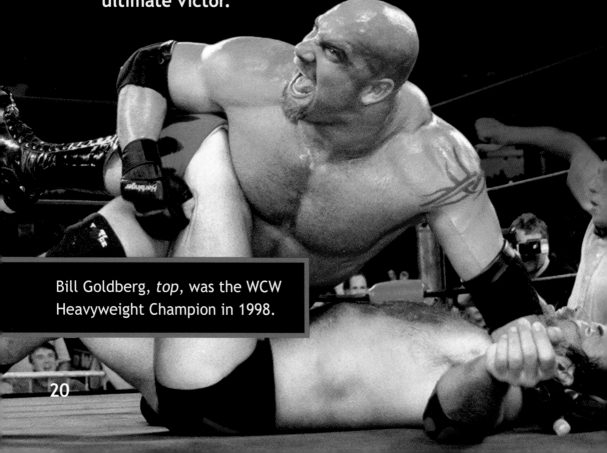

Bill Goldberg, *top*, was the WCW Heavyweight Champion in 1998.

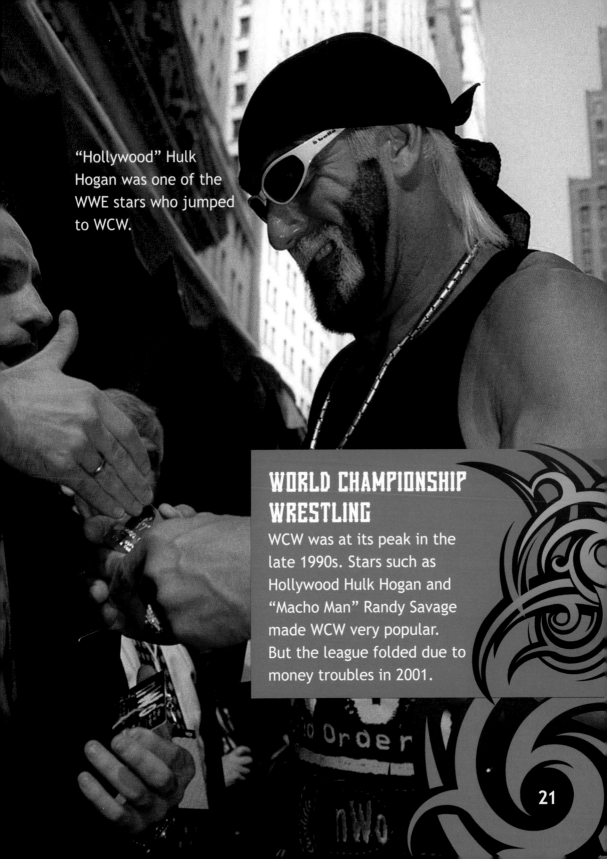

"Hollywood" Hulk Hogan was one of the WWE stars who jumped to WCW.

WORLD CHAMPIONSHIP WRESTLING

WCW was at its peak in the late 1990s. Stars such as Hollywood Hulk Hogan and "Macho Man" Randy Savage made WCW very popular. But the league folded due to money troubles in 2001.

THREE

DAY JOBS

The biggest stars in pro wrestling make millions of dollars. But most pro wrestlers earn far less. Those who work for small promotions or in house shows usually get paid by the match. It's not enough money to live on. So most pro wrestlers have other jobs. By day they work in offices, on loading docks, or at gyms. At night, they transform into heels and babyfaces and hit the mat.

Some wrestlers, such as Kane, can make extra money by signing autographs, but many other wrestlers have to work a second job.

TWO

TRAINING SCHOOLS

Wrestlers don't just show up and achieve stardom. It takes a lot of hard work. Many of them train in special wrestling schools. They learn the techniques in the ring and how to act outside the ring. Most wrestlers start out in developmental leagues. There, they master their moves. They create their characters. And if they do well, they get their shot on the big stage.

Aspiring pro wrestlers pick up tips and learn their moves in wrestling schools.

ONE

INJURIES

Pro wrestlers sometimes seem invincible. It appears as if nothing can hurt them. But that's not really true. Injuries are a big problem in pro wrestling. The wear and tear of wrestlers slamming, diving, and beating on each other takes its toll. Many of them struggle with back injuries. Others suffer broken bones. Head injuries are among the most serious problems. Concussions can cause permanent brain damage.

John Cena flies high in a 2015 match.

Brock Lesnar, *top*, pounds Randy Orton into submission at SummerSlam 2016.

Wrestlers like John Cena, *left*, and The Rock are under a lot of pressure to look and perform their best.

Drug abuse goes along with injuries. Some wrestlers become addicted to painkillers. Others turn to muscle-building steroids to keep up their appearance. These drugs can lead to health problems, depression, and even death.

The action in the ring is thrilling. The personalities are larger than life. But pro wrestlers are people, like anyone else. And their bodies pay the price for what they do.

The Undertaker throws Shawn Michaels over the ropes in a particularly violent match at WrestleMania 26 in 2010.

GLOSSARY

BABYFACE
A wrestler seen as a good guy; also called a face.

DEVELOPMENTAL LEAGUE
A small league where wrestlers can learn their craft.

HEEL
A wrestler seen as a villain.

HOUSE SHOW
A traveling wrestling show that is not broadcast on TV.

KAYFABE
A term used to describe the antics of on-screen characters.

RIVALRY
A long-standing, intense, and often emotional competition between two people or teams.

TURNBUCKLE
A device used to connect the ropes of a wrestling ring.

FOR MORE INFORMATION

BOOKS

Kortemeier, Todd. *Superstars of WWE*. Mankato, MN: Amicus High Interest, 2016.

Scheff, Matt. *Pro Wrestling's Greatest Faces*. Minneapolis, MN: Abdo Publishing, 2017.

WEBSITES

To learn more about pro wrestling, visit booklinks.abdopublishing.com. These links are routinely monitored and updated to provide the most current information available.

INDEX

ABOUT THE AUTHOR

Matt Scheff is an artist and author living in Alaska. He enjoys mountain climbing, deep-sea fishing, and curling up with his two Siberian huskies to watch wrestling.